R.C. NIKKI

So You Want a Dog in Your Life...

For Future Dog owners, Things you need to know

INICIO Publishing Corp.

This book was professionally typeset on Reedsy.
Find out more at reedsy.com

Contents

Introduction

So you want to be a dog owner...we all do or did at one point in time or another. Whether it is from meeting a friend's dog in person, passing along a pet store and seeing them through a glass window, taking a walk in your neighborhood and watching dogs run around the dog park. You thought to yourself, "Oh, How cute, I want a dog too..." This book serves to help you decide.

Dogs are everywhere! Even when you don't own one, you probably live near people that do. So what is stopping you from getting one? This book is meant to give you the honest truth of what to expect when you get a puppy or a dog. Maybe it is time for you to get a dog, maybe its not the right time. Aside from time, there are other factors you need to consider. Lets be honest here, not everyone deserves to have a dog. We have all seen the brutality on videos online. I recall the one where a bunch of kids poured gasoline on a living animal and set it on fire. There are definitely some inhumane owners out there that chain their dogs to trees days on end, or keep them outside in the scorching heat without clean water supply. So what makes us good dog parents?

Hi there! My name is Nikki and I have lived with dog companions most of my life. Most of my friends have dogs of their own. Regardless of their size, breed, energy level or personalities, they are definitely a wonderful additional family member I needed in my life. There has been many experiences, both good and bad that triggered me to write this book. I would like to share a few tips, some educational information and some realistic considerations you should have when deciding on getting a puppy or a dog. I want to share some very personal experiences with you all and hope you can do better than I as a new dog parent. I also wanted to dive into topics usually people shy away from when deciding to incorporate a puppy into their lives.

With that being said, happy reading! Cheers!

-R.C. Nikki

Financial Black Hole

Know what you are getting yourself into.

You should know that puppies can cost a fortune! It is a commitment of roughly 10-15 years depending on the size of the puppy. Know that once committed, puppies are easily influenced by it's owner and can be scarred for life if they are neglected or abused. Think of all the adoption dogs that came to be there due to negligence, poor financial background, or even subjected to abuse. Having dogs is like training to have kids one day. Are you ready mentally, financially and physically prepared for that?

According to AKC.org[1], the average costs by dog size are as follows:

- Small dog: $15,051
- Medium dog: $15,782
- Large dog: $14,480

When you see the numbers, what are you thinking? Perhaps, where does it all go? How is it possible? Well the answer to that is broken into the following:

---

[1] https://www.akc.org/expert-advice/lifestyle/how-much-spend-on-dog-in-lifetime/
#:~:text=Including%20all%20possible%20expenses%2C%20they,%2C%20breed%2
C%20and%20services%20required.

First, let's look at some statistical findings from Finmasters.com. During the pandemic, more and more people are getting pets because humans are social creatures and lacking any social activity can cause major damages to our mental health. Hopefully, that is not the only reason but the current statistics place about 90.5 million households have a pet at home.[2] That is roughly 2 out of 3 households in the United States has at least one pet friend.[3] This begs the question, how much money did we spend on pets yearly? In the United States, roughly $123.6 billion were spent on pet products and services.[4] The most pet spending occurred are veterinarians visits, food and supplies. Dog health is very important and like a child, must be care for constantly. One mishap can lead to months or years of ongoing medical treatment that can be a financial burden. Because of this, purchasing of pet insurance is on the incline. More and more people are set to spurge on pet health insurance. I, myself found a pet insurance that covers physical therapy because how expensive dog therapy treatments were. Pet insurance became a topic of discussion at every dog park date and more of them I meet either were planning on getting pet insurance or already have. The number of insured pets were 26% higher in 2021 compared to 2020 and 63% higher

[2] *Pet industry market size, Trends & Ownership Statistics.* American Pet Products Association. (n.d.). Retrieved September 3, 2022, from https://www.americanpetproducts.org/press _industrytrends.asp

[3] *Pet industry market size, Trends & Ownership Statistics.* American Pet Products Association. (n.d.). Retrieved September 3, 2022, from https://www.americanpetproducts.org/press _industrytrends.asp

[4] *Pet industry market size, Trends & Ownership Statistics.* American Pet Products Association. (n.d.). Retrieved September 3, 2022, from https://www.americanpetproducts.org/press _industrytrends.asp

compared to 2018.[5]

The APPA, (American Pet Products Association) breaks down the sales in 2021. For our purposes, the top three highest categories spent are listed below:[6]

1. Pet food and treats ($50.0 billion in sales)
2. Supplies, Live animals and OTC Medicine (29.8 billion in sales)
3. Vet Care & Product Sales (34.3 billion in sales)

According to Finmasters.com, pet owners spend roughly $1,480 a year or roughly $50/month on their canine friends.[7] I have come to calculate that I spend WAYY more than that on a monthly basis. I pulled some data from my financial data and within a year I spend roughly $4000 on my dogs.

"How did I manage to do that?" Over the years, I have lived with dogs of every size, various personalities and different energy levels. The smallest breed I had were Yorkshire Terriers, - Yorkies for short. I had a boy and a girl. Yorkies are supposed to be a territorial breed, but mine were so friendly with strangers, I wouldn't be surprised if they played with a burglar instead of barking for help. Reason I bring this up is

---

[5] Ciochia, A.-I. (2022, July 25). *Pet spending statistics (2022): How much do Americans spend on pets?* FinMasters. Retrieved September 3, 2022, from https://finmasters.com/pet-spending-statistics/#:~:text=U.S.%20pet%20owners%20reportedly%20spend,to%20vet%20visits%20and%20grooming.

[6] *Pet industry market size, Trends & Ownership Statistics.* American Pet Products Association. (n.d.). Retrieved September 3, 2022, from https://www.americanpetproducts.org/press_industrytrends.asp

[7] Ciochia, A.-I. (2022, July 25). *Pet spending statistics (2022): How much do Americans spend on pets?* FinMasters. Retrieved September 3, 2022, from https://finmasters.com/pet-spending-statistics/#:~:text=U.S.%20pet%20owners%20reportedly%20spend,to%20vet%20visits%20and%20grooming.

because of their size, smaller breeds tend to have joint issues. Medication for dogs, physical therapy, joint supplements, specialty dog beds can add up.

If you decide to feed your dog kibbles versus real food, that will make a different in monthly spending. My first puppy came from a pet store, I was 19, lived alone and passing by those puppy eyes, the adorable tiny litter of pups running around the store front gated window, in their own feces and urine, I still bought him. I wish I had learned what I know now and I now share this information with all of you.

There are different a large price range when it comes to food. Some cost $5 others cost $40, some even cost $100 or more. Cheaper does not mean better for sure. What new dog owners tend to buy are kibbles or soft foods. When I was a first time dog owner, I bought kibbles, a 40 lb bag would cost about $100 dollars and last roughly 1.5 months. That alone is already more than $50 dollars a month. When you learn more about food quality for pets, veterinary diets and healthier real food options cost even more. According to Pawtracks.com, the average veterinary diets can cost roughly $100 a month.[8] We have not even added in dog treats yet!

Pet owners need to be made aware that it is not good to leave the dry dog food out all day long. This will attract unnecessary critters as dry pet food contains nutrients as well as chemicals. By leaving dog food out all day, whenever they want to nibble on something, they tend to over eat. AKC.org mentioned that almost 34% of adult dogs are obese and there is a 2 year difference in lifespan compared to a normal weighed dog..[9]

---

[8] LaFrank, G. (2021, May 21). *This is how much you should budget for Dog Food Monthly.* PawTracks. Retrieved September 3, 2022, from https://www.pawtracks.com/dogs/dog-food-cost-monthly/

[9] Burke, A. (2021, May 27). *How long do dogs live?* American Kennel Club. Retrieved September 3, 2022, from https://www.akc.org/expert-advice/health/how-long-do-dogs-live/

Questions to ask yourself in regards to finance:

1. How much money are you willing to spend on your dog?
2. What size dog would be best suited for you?
3. Will you give your pet health insurance?
4. Are you going to feed your pet kibbles or real food?

After answering the questions above, let the information sink in, think about it and think about it some more and if you have no financial cap on how much money can be spent then proceed to the next chapter. If you have doubts on if you can afford a dog, I suggest find other ways to be around more dogs instead. Money, time and commitment is a must when handling new canine furry friends.

Lifespan of a dog

Commitment of a decade, that's what this is. Unlike felines, who are self sufficient, canines require much more attention, like a child. When deciding to get a dog for the first time, one thing to keep in mind is the importance of the lifespan of the dog. Obviously its not the only measure of choosing a decade long companion, but it should be talked about. Lifespan can vary based on breed and weight. In the last chapter, we spoke about the obesity in canines and how it affects their overall lifespan. Losing an average of 2 years of life due to obesity is alarming. So lets shed some light on the topic-Lifespan of a dog.

According to AKC.org, smaller breeds can live longer than larger breeds.[10] I always thought the reverse so its interesting to find this out while doing research. Apparently, this is due to the accelerated growth spurt of large canines. In case you are not a science person, here's a little science:

The cell cycle is the process in which the cell replicates and makes two new cells. There are different stages of the process, namely G1, S, G2 and M phase. [11] While it is more complex than described here, that

[10] Burke, A. (2021, May 27). *How long do dogs live?* American Kennel Club. Retrieved September 3, 2022, from https://www.akc.org/expert-advice/health/how-long-do-dogs-live/

[11] *Cell cycle.* Genome.gov. (n.d.). Retrieved September 3, 2022, from https://www.genome.gov/genetics-glossary/Cell-Cycle

is a different nonfiction book. Just know that while replication occurs, there are multiple internal controls called checkpoints that regulates the process to go to move forward. These cell cycle checkpoints monitor the order and integrity of all major phases of cell growth.[12] When rapid growth occurs, more likely than not, the checkpoints are no longer functioning correctly leading to hyperactivity, mutations and lead to the rise of cancer cells. (This is why accelerated growth may lead to shorter lifespans in larger dogs– very sad.)

Back to the point:

According to AKC.org, (the American Kennel Club), the average lifespan for smaller breeds are roughly 10-15 years. The general consensus for what is considered a small breed is determined by weight. After researching various sites, smaller breeds averagely weigh around 20 lbs (+/- 5lbs). [13]

So why choose a smaller breed? Why did I pick a small breed?

Who hasn't watched Reese Whitherspoon's Legally Blond growing up. Who didn't want a pet they could toss in their bag and carry everywhere? I know I did!

Smaller breeds are well suited for the city life and smaller apartments. In a city like New York, it is difficult to keep a large dog in a 500 square foot apartment, whom need extra space to roam and burn off excess energy. Overall, smaller breeds tend to eat less quantity compared to larger breeds. This makes them more cost efficient compared. Another reason to pick smaller breeds is the amount of fur shedding is much less.

---

[12] Barnum KJ, O'Connell MJ. Cell cycle regulation by checkpoints. Methods Mol Biol. 2014;1170:29-40. doi: 10.1007/978-1-4939-0888-2_2. PMID: 24906307; PMCID: PMC4990352.

[13] Burke, A. (2021, May 27). *How long do dogs live?* American Kennel Club. Retrieved August 28, 2022, from https://www.akc.org/expert-advice/health/how-long-do-dogs-live/

If you have allergies to animals, likely chance that you pick a breed that is hypoallergenic would be a smaller breed.

Why not?

Although they are smaller bundles of joy, they do eat more frequently than larger breeds. So they may need more attention to meal times since they require more caloric intake. Another important fact to mention is that smaller breeds are more accident prone and can be costly if they fall from high places. Pet owners with small children should reconsider getting a small breed. It would be both dishearten if the dog gets stepped on or the child gets bitten by a yappy pup. Smaller breeds are more fragile beings compared to a human child, but likewise, it lowers the chance of risk. According to Hillspet.com, the top three most aggressive breeds are all from small breeds group.[14] (Mainly the three in bold). Although not all display aggressive behaviors, certain type of dogs get a bad rep. Usually, its due to pet parents that don't see the aggression as harmful and immediately fix the behavior. This leads to UN-trained, UN-socialized pets that lash out uncontrolled. This is why they can't handle being in public, in dog parks and anywhere else that is not your home. YES! Pet Moms and Pet Dads, this is your doing! Regardless, obedience training and socialization is needed for all sizes. Below is a short list of smaller breeds, which came from Purina.com. Of course it is not limited to just these couple bullet points, but its a few to start your research on.

- **Chihuahua**
- Terriers like **Jack Russell**, Boston, Border, Russell, Manchester,

---

[14] *Small dog breeds - big personalities: Hill's pet.* Hill's Pet Nutrition. (n.d.). Retrieved September 3, 2022, from https://www.hillspet.com/dog-care/behavior-appearance/comprehensive-guide-to-small-dog-breeds

Norwich, and Yorkshires
· Spaniels like Cavalier King Charles, English toy
· Pomeranian
· Bichon Frise
· Beagles
· Corgies
· **Dachshund**
· French Bulldogs
· Havanese
· Lhasa apso
· Mini Schnauzer
· Pekingese
· Pugs
· Shih tzu
· Cavapoos

Between the small breeds and the large breeds, the best-est of both worlds are medium size breeds. (Definitely a personal opinion- my reason being is that they have medium hand size poops, easily picked up from the streets!). Medium size dogs tend to be higher in energy compared to smaller breeds and some of the smartest dog breeds belong to this group. They are perfect size for snuggles and hugs. As Goldilocks would say, "not too big and not too small, it's just right!"[15] Below is a compilation of some of the most popular medium size dog breeds from Sprucepets.com. [16] Most breeds on this list are fairly playful, active and intelligent, they are mostly working, herding and hunting breeds.

---

[15] Marshall, J. (2013). *Goldilocks and the three bears*. Walker Books.

[16] Stregowski, J. (2022, February 8). *20 popular medium-size dog breeds*. The Spruce Pets. Retrieved September 3, 2022, from https://www.thesprucepets.com/medium-dog-bre eds-4582517

- Terriers like American Staffordshire, Bull Terriers, Kerry Blue, Soft coated Wheaten,
- Australian Cattle Dog
- Australian Shepherd, Mini American Shepherds
- Basset Hound
- Beagles
- Bearded Collie
- Border Collie
- Spaniels like Boykin, Cocker, English Springer
- Bulldog
- Dalmatian
- Pembroke Welsh Corgi
- Schnauzers
- Whippet

According to AKC.org, large dogs have an average lifespan of 8-12 years. When choosing your companion, it is best to keep this in mind. The leading cause of death in large dogs are due to cancer. Not only do larger dogs live a shorter life, upkeep is much more costly as well. Because of their built, they require larger portions for both food and space. Pet supplies also add up because they require larger toys, snacks, beds, etc. Most common traits of larger dogs I have seen are loyal and protective. They tend to be great family dogs and will keep their pack safe. More research is needed based on breed to better find a suitable canine for you and your family.

Below is a list of large dog companions from AKC.org.[17]

---

[17] Sassafras Lowrey, C. T. D. I. (2021, November 19). *World's largest dog breeds: 16 giant dogs.* American Kennel Club. Retrieved September 3, 2022, from https://www.akc.org/expert-advice/dog-breeds/16-largest-dog-breeds/

- Anatolian Shepherd
- Bernese Mountain Dog
- Terriers like Black Russian,
- Bullmastiff, Mastiff, Neapolitan Mastiff, Tibetan Mastiff
- Dogue de Bordeaux
- Cane Corso
- Great Dane
- Great Pyrenees
- Irish Wolfhound
- Leonberger
- Newfoundland
- Saint Bernard
- Scottish Deerhound

Regardless of size, all dogs are trainable. The time and effort you put in will determine how well behaved they can be. So why did I choose to talk about lifespan? A decade may seem like it is a very long time, however your pet's life is actually quite short compared to yours. I have experienced many solemn moments. When a dog passes on, and you decide to do it the right way, you would bring them to your vet for cremation. This can also be priced based on weight. So the heavier the dog, the higher the cremation costs are. If you have chosen to get a dog, know that their entire lives circles around you. Don't look back and regret the days you left them alone when you went on dates. Don't regret giving them away to family to care for them because you got tired of the responsibility. A decade is just a blink of an eye. Once they are gone, you'd wish you had spent more time with them. Do right by your furry companion. Give them the quality time they deserve.

Now that you have a list of each breed based on size, its time to answer some questions:

1. In reality, how much space are you willing to share with your new furry companion?
2. What traits are you looking for in a canine?
3. Do you have allergies to dog dander?
4. In reality, how much time do you have to spare in a day for training and socializing them correctly?
5. Does their lifespan matter to you now?

You now have a clearer picture of what you are getting yourself into. Dedication and time is needed, a decade's worth. All breeds can be trained, time and effort is needed from both you and your canine friend. Put the effort in and it will be worth it. All you can do is direct them in a happier, more fulfilling life. Now let's go to the next chapter.

Breeders versus Pet Stores

Where should I get my puppy?

"But Nikki, the Pet store is right down the street!"

"It's so convenient..."

"I got a GREAT deal at the pet store!"

"But Nikki, this pet store delivers right to my door! How amazing is that?"

According to the Humanesociety.org, pet stores rarely get their dogs from breeders. Truth is that when you buy puppies from a breeder, they will ask you a series of questions to make sure that their puppies are going to good homes, that you are capable of taking care of them; that your home allows pets. Responsible breeders usually would not sell their puppies to pet stores. Why is that? Well, if you had too many mouths to feed and children you can't take care of, would you want them to go to a good home or a bad one? Same concept, breeders want to ensure their puppies go to a proper home.

AKC.org also has a code of ethics which prohibits or discourages breeders from selling to pet stores. Usually pet stores are supplied by puppy mills that mass produce puppies for monetary gains. Forbes also did an article on The Humane Society of the United States has conducted several hidden-camera investigations to showing that many of the breeding facilities that supply pet stores are mills.

New owners, please don't forsake your new puppy's life due to convenience. If you ever seen a dog in pain, it's heart wrenching. If you have seen a loved one lose their pet, you remain silent because no words will express the sympathies. If you choose to get a pet, their lives are in your hands. By contributing to pet stores, they continue to remain rampant. According to Andrew Nibley, 99 % of all pet stores still use puppies from puppy mills. It is a simple concept of supply and demand. If people stop buying from pet stores, puppy mills would cease to exist.[18]

They don't care about the puppies, they care more about the $$$$. Many older pet stores get their pups from puppy mills. When this occurs, large quantities of dogs are bred under stress and pumped out like factory products, even when there are defects. Usually pet stores would have a $ back guarantee or equal exchange. This is why you as the consumer end up paying hefty prices for lack of a better phrase- damaged goods. Let that sink in for a moment, but honestly, I encourage all dog seeking companions to stay away from pet stores.

Puppies are in better health if they came from breeders. I applaud all new dog owners to either purchase from a breeder or save dogs from the animal shelter. If the breeders are not available in your area because chances are, the breeds you desire might reside in a different state, there will be a transportation fee for drop off to the airport. If you could please consider checking your local animal shelter and sign up for adoptions instead, it would save canines from death before their time. Over 3 million adoptable dogs and cats are euthanized in shelters every year. [19]

Saving a dog's life from termination before their time would be a

---

[18] John, A. S. (2012, April 26). *Where *not* to buy a dog: The pet store connection to the business of puppy mills.* Forbes. Retrieved August 28, 2022, from https://www.forbes.com/sites/allenstjohn/2012/02/22/where-not-to-buy-a-dog-the-pet-store-connection-to-the-business-of-puppy-mills/?sh=534d725d1d1c

[19] Pet Industry Market Size and Ownership Statistics, https://www.americanpetproducts.org/press_industrytrends.asp (accessed January 13, 2020).

heroic thing to do. It is like giving them a second chance at a better life. Although, shelter dogs may have behavior problems, ultimately that can be fixed with a little bit of love and time. Shelter dogs become shelter dogs can be due to a number of reasons. Abusive dog owners that don't bother feeding them a proper meal, or hits the animal. Others are due to the lack of financial means to continue keeping them at home. Regardless of which, dogs can develop behavior problems unrelated to the actual action. This type of training would be more independent of the dog's history and time to undo the past would be dependent on that as well.

Reasons to not use Pet Stores:

1. Because the large pools of animals are stuffed into small glass window spacing, usually the animals contract ear mites from one another. If you see constant scratching at the ears, it's possible they have ear mites. Best get it checked out at the vet. My first puppy came from the pet store. I was young and didn't know any better. All it took was a walk pass a pet store to me ultimately putting $1,300 into my credit card adding to my list of debts.

2. According to ASPCA.org, dogs are crammed into dirty, over packed cages that are denied healthy foods, clean water and basic veterinary care. Mother dogs are bred without screening for diseases.[20] This is not so untrue as I have also witnessed it on many occasions passing by pet stores. The puppies are laying in their own urine and the shredded news papers were no longer just printed paper.

3. Since the pup's health condition is in question, puppy mill puppies can develop health and behavioral problems that are costly to

---

[20] 3 shady things pet stores don't want you to know. ASPCA. (n.d.). Retrieved September 3, 2022, from https://www.aspca.org/news/3-shady-things-pet-stores-dont-want-you-know#:~:text=Dogs%20are%20usually%20crammed%20into,rest%20or%20screening%20for%20diseases.

treat. [21] When you purchase an animal at the pet store, it does not come with any documentation for vaccines, blood work, hereditary genetic testing, stool culture results, eye testing, etc. You do not know what you are getting. I can attest to this as well, my first puppy had no paperwork, literally paid and go. Picked up the dog and the receipt and took the train home.

4. Don't be fooled by the fancy words pet stores throw at you. Almost anyone can state that their breeders are USDA-licensed or have AKC registration. However, this does not guarantee their well being. The standards of USDA are low or still fails short of what pet parents would consider humane. AKC registry solely states that the puppies parents both had AKC papers. [22]

5. Pet stores sometimes have payment plans that are unethical and down right ridiculous. Pet leasing or financing, allows customers to pay for the puppy in a monthly basis and can cost more than the animal's original price. In fact, with a lease, you are not the actual owner until the lease is completely paid off. [23]

6. By contributing to Pet Stores, Puppy mills continue to exist. You as a consumer is doing much more harm than good if you decide to get an animal from the pet store. Please reconsider and share this

---

[21] *3 shady things pet stores don't want you to know.* ASPCA. (n.d.). Retrieved September 3, 2022, from https://www.aspca.org/news/3-shady-things-pet-stores-dont-want-you-know#:~:text=Dogs%20are%20usually%20crammed%20into,rest%20or%20screening%20for%20diseases.

[22] *3 shady things pet stores don't want you to know.* ASPCA. (n.d.). Retrieved September 3, 2022, from https://www.aspca.org/news/3-shady-things-pet-stores-dont-want-you-know#:~:text=Dogs%20are%20usually%20crammed%20into,rest%20or%20screening%20for%20diseases.

[23] *3 shady things pet stores don't want you to know.* ASPCA. (n.d.). Retrieved September 3, 2022, from https://www.aspca.org/news/3-shady-things-pet-stores-dont-want-you-know#:~:text=Dogs%20are%20usually%20crammed%20into,rest%20or%20screening%20for%20diseases.

information with anyone that wants a dog.

If you haven't heard of this shady business pet stores are in before, now you have a little more knowledge to better determine your decisions. Which will it be, would you still consider a pet store or would you choose to go to a breeder or a animal shelter? At the end of the day, the choice is still yours to make. I hope you will contribute to the betterment of the bigger picture.

Veterinary Doctor Visits

Finding the right Vet for you.

One important experience I need to share with you is to always be sure to look for a veterinarian that allows you to be inside the examination room with your furry friend. You should not be forced to sit outside the waiting area. Vet visits are very much like a child's doctor's visit. It can be scary and traumatizing for the dog to visit a stranger's place without you, especially when getting shots or other blood works done. Dog's have a great sense of smell, but more than that, they have really good recall memory, especially when it comes to pain. After a couple monthly vet visits for vaccines and consultation, going back to the Vet yearly has been more difficult with my dogs. They know exactly where you are taking them and sometimes they refuse to enter the office altogether.

As a new pup owner, check for deals a Veterinary Clinic may offer for new puppies clients. Packages usually cover 1-2 years of age, making consultations, vaccines and boosters much cheaper than regular visits. I would also recommend having pet insurance as it can help pay back parts of your payment to the vet. Unlike human doctor visits, dog insurance pays you out and not the Veterinary Clinic . You have to pay the full charge directly after your visit at the clinic and then claim your dog insurance for payment after you get back. It is fairly simple, and consist of using a phone to take a picture of the bill, which is called a claim and request for claim reimbursement. Most pet insurances are roughly $50-$60 per month. They include a deductible or an out-of-pocket expense that could be subjected to less reimbursement. As every policy is different, please shop around and find the best one for you. After all the pet insurances I have tried out, it is better to not expect full reimbursement. I learned that even with the best plan, there are still certain deductibles that will not be paid in full.

Why get dog insurance? You never know what could happen. One day your pup could be fine, then a week long diarrhea...which could be okay for a human, but a week-long issue with diarrhea is fatal for a puppy. Coming back from the Veterinary Clinic for that was super expensive, like $600 expensive! and yes, if you are wondering if this happened to me? It did! Don't settle for a Veterinarian that is close to you without first checking to see if they are good doctors. Make sure that you are comfortable with them first and that they are willing to answer all your questions and concerns and not just pushing you out the door. If you haven't found anyone, do some shopping around. Another way of getting this type of information is at the dog park. Usually, dog owners would take they dogs out to run the enclosed park unleashed. Dog owners can shed some light on where to go and chances are you probably made a new best friend who understands your concerns.

It is also a good idea to know where your local animal hospital is located and that your pet insurance covers ER visits. If any emergencies occur, it is best to have the information on hand. One example I can recall, is taking the dog to the mall and having their paw pad rip off because it got stuck on the escalator. When you are in a panic and blood is gushing out, you never want to be spending the time searching for an ER. Instead, the hands should be keeping pressure on the wound to stop further blood loss. So an extra tip for you, don't let your dogs (small or big) step in an escalator or even the metal grids on the streets.

Well behaved or Spoiled Rotten?

Do you want obedience or are you ready to spoil your dog daily?

As mentioned in chapter 2, bad behavior for animals are due to the negligence of their human owners. The worst you can do is blame the dog because:

1. Usually the misdeed has taken place long before you realize the issue
2. Dogs have really good memory when it comes to what upsets you. So if you need to retrain a mishap, do it properly or they will link the treatment you dealt to them directly to you.
3. If the owner doesn't correct the behavior, it will never be known to the dog that it is a bad behavior.

If you don't put in the effort to lay the ground work, is it really the dog's fault when it chews your favorite pair of heels? Your Nintendo switch gaming controller? What about if they missed the wee wee pad multiple times and caused your wooden floors to rot? (Yes, urine is acidic and can breakdown wood if not cleaned directly after urination.) What if they are teething and chews on your furniture? Or pees on your furniture? Dogs in the wild do not need permission to do any of that. So if kept UN-trained, and UN-socialized, they will do whatever they want. Essentially, they become the alpha of the pack. Having experience with so many dogs in my life have definitely refined my training process with my pack. From personal experience, you either can be a tough cookie and be the leader of the pack and train them well or they are the leader and you are the follower.

As canines are closely related to wolves, dogs tend to follow similar suits of command like a pack. In a wolf pack, there is only one Alpha dog and the rest are Betas. When meeting your dog for the first time, signs of a follower would be to not stare at you directly; when permissive, will have their heads down. Based on my own expertise, you can either fail to train your puppy and they will be very spoiled and on top of you; don't learn commands or queues and does whatever they want regardless of your frustrations and complaints.

When learning to live together, it is important to understand that it is not just the puppy that needs to learn to adapt, the human needs to learn to live with a dog as well. When properly trained, dogs are your most loyalist followers and they will react and protect you as they see fit. They will learn their boundaries on where they can go, what they are allowed to chew on and more so, how to behave the way you want them to. So as a dog owner, you should know what you are comfortable with. Are they allowed on the bed, the furniture, etc. Thus obedience or spoiled, this is something you can decide when you first get the puppy. And yes, those loving, adorable puppy eyes are going to sucker you into being passive. Just like there are different types of parents, there are different types of dog owners as well. Which type do you want to be?

For obedience training, you would want to start your pup as early as you get them. This way they have more time to learn and adapt. Know that training sessions should be short because that actually drains their energy much faster than physical exercise. Repetition and patience is key.

Pup Socializing and Separation Anxiety

Socializing your puppy, why its important and how how to familiarize them?

Like newborn babies, puppies need to acclimate to a new environment. They need to experience, touch, and smell new things. After getting a puppy, don't leave them alone in the house or apartment by themselves for too long. Puppies like babies require constant attention and correction at the moments notice. There are tons of socializing lists on the web but the best one I came across belongs to Ultimatepuppy.com, called the "Ultimate Puppy Worksheet"[24]. The worksheet provides an in-depth list of things your puppy should experience early on in life to get them comfortable in all surroundings.

Unless you work and live at home, most of us-single or partnered, are required to head into the office 4-5 days a week. The duration of time we usually leave the dog home alone is 40+ hours a week. If this is you, do train your puppy to stay home alone slowly. Canines are emotion creatures that become very attached to their pack. It is always better to leave them with family if you have to leave for 8+ hours if not properly trained. When canines develop separation anxiety, the damage could be

---

[24] *A social schedule – puppy socialization checklist.* Ultimate Puppy. (2021, June 8). Retrieved September 4, 2022, from https://ultimatepuppy.com/socialization/puppy-socializatio n-checklist/

monstrous.

What is separation anxiety and how do you know if your puppy is exhibiting that behavior? For starters, they become disruptive and even destructive when left alone. Separation anxiety occurs when their owners are separated from them and they become distressed and upset. Have you ever left for 30 minutes to get groceries and come back to a room full of torn up pillows with the stuffing all over the room? what about scratching through a wooden door to get out? These escape attempts are common with distressed dogs. What about the excessive chewing that occurs only when you step out of the apartment?

Below is a list of common symptoms of Separation Anxiety taken from ASPCA.org. [25]

1. Urination and defecation
2. Barking and howling
3. Destruction
4. Attempting to Escape
5. Pacing back and forth
6. Coprophagi

Why do dogs develop separation anxiety? There's no one definite answer. There's multiple. Depending on the history of the dog you are getting, if from the shelter, could have past trauma or behavior problems. When you have multiple dogs, the loss of one will change the behavior of the others. If you are adopting a dog, separation anxiety may happen due to previous abandonment issues they faced. You must start training them early and in short intervals gradually getting longer and longer. The earlier you can knock out the various types of experiences the better.

---

[25] *Separation anxiety.* ASPCA. (n.d.). Retrieved September 4, 2022, from https://www.aspc a.org/pet-care/dog-care/common-dog-behavior-issues/separation-anxiety

This includes brushing their teeth and clipping their nails. They need to get comfortable with you touching the outside and the inside their mouths and holding their paws. When they get older, it will be more difficult to do this if you are introducing it later on in life.

Decisions, Decisions..

So you finally finished the book. I hope now, you have a little more confidence in your decision moving forward. As rambunctious as dogs can be, obedience training will help with poor behavior, along with proper socializing and healthy diet. All dogs have their personalities and all they really want to do is please you. Whether this book has deter you from getting a puppy currently or has confirmed your everlasting confidence. I wish you the best journey forward. It is definitely rewarding to have dogs in my life and I hope you will feel the same way too. I have learned a lot and I think I am better equipped to have my own child because of them. Not the same, but is a long commitment just like a baby. I would recommend it for anyone at least once in their lifetime to experience all the joys and pains of this connection.

Printed in Great Britain
by Amazon